Pavo Explores The Solar System

Dana Rowe

www.TotalPublishingAndMedia.com

ISBN 978-1-937829-67-4

Dedicated to my favorite little astronaut, Evan I Love you to the edge of the universe and back!

This is Pavo, a silly slobbery alien from Alpha Centauri Bb who believes humans really do exist and plans on exploring the solar system to prove it!

Explorer Facts:

Pavo is a constellation in the southern sky. Its name is Latin for peacock.

Alpha Centauri Bb is a planet in a nearby system and appears to look identical to Earth but is still too hot to live on.

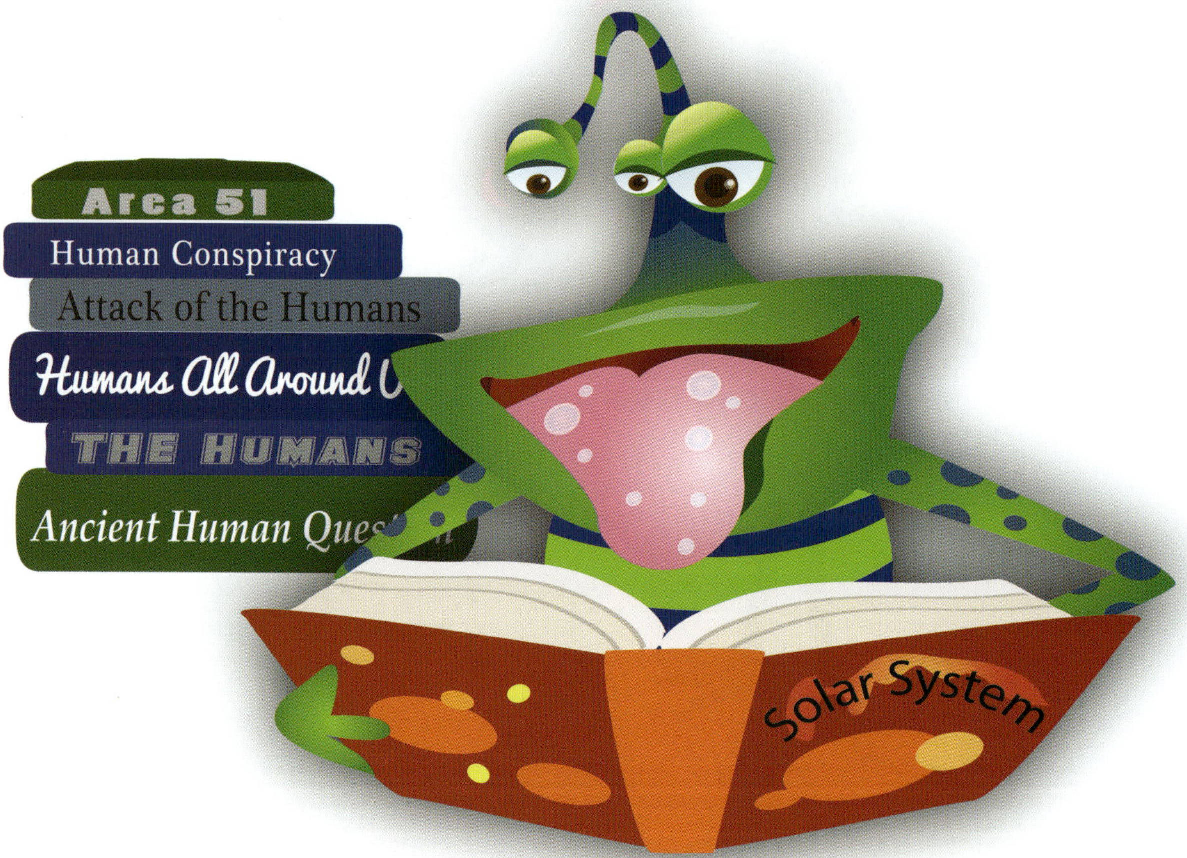
Area 51
Human Conspiracy
Attack of the Humans
Humans All Around
THE HUMANS
Ancient Human Ques
Solar System

Pavo loves to look at the beautiful stars, especially the Sun. Will you help Pavo explore the Solar System and find the Sun?

Explorer Facts:

The closest Earthlike planet is over 120 trillion miles away. Even if you were traveling 11 miles a second the journey would still take over 350,000 years to complete!

Count down with Pavo!
5,4,3,2,1
Blast off!!!!!

"No wonder Pluto is a dwarf planet, it's too small! Where would you live? Where would you play? No, no, no there are no humans on Pluto and my favorite star is still much, much too far away!"

Pluto Explorer Facts:

Pluto is smaller than Earth's moon.

If you weigh 50 lbs. on Earth you would weigh 3.3 lbs. on Pluto.

Pluto orbits the sun every 248 earth years.

Pluto has 4 moons.

Great Neptune! I'm about to be blown away!!!

Do you think humans could live on such a windy planet?

Neptune Explorer Facts:

Neptune is the windiest planet up to 1,200 mph.

Neptune has 6 rings and 13 moons.

If you weigh 50 lbs on Earth you would weigh 56 lbs on Neptune.

1 year on Neptune equals 165 Earth years. 1 day on Neptune equals 16 Earth hours.

Who turned out the lights!? Brrrr! Uranus is freezing and I can't see a thing! This planet needs to get moving already!

Uranus Explorer Facts:

    Uranus rotates so slow that one side is in darkness for up to 42 years.

    Uranus has 2 rings and 27 moons.

    1 year on Uranus equals 84 Earth Years and 1 day on Uranus equals 17 hours.

    If you weigh 50 lbs. on Earth you would weigh 44 lbs. on Uranus.

    Uranus is the ice planet at -407 °F.

On Saturn I'm the greatest spaceship driver since Snail Burnhardt!

Saturn Explorer Facts:

    Saturn has 53 moons and 7 rings.

    Saturns rings are 169,800 miles wide and a half a mile to 2 miles thick.

    If you weigh 50 lbs. on Earth you would weigh 53 lbs. on Saturn.

Either I'm shrinking or Jupiter is the largest planet in this Solar System!

Can you find Pavo?

Jupiter Explorer Facts:

    Jupiter has 50 moons.

    Temperatures on Jupiter can reach up to 17,000 ºF.

    The core of Jupiter is the size of Earth and reaches temperatures of 64,000 ºF.

    1 year on Jupiter equals 12 years on Earth and 1 day on Jupiter equals 10 hours on Earth.

    If you weigh 50 lbs. on Earth you would weigh 118 lbs. on Jupiter.

The Great Red Spot is one ShOcKiNg place to visit!

Jupiter Explorer Facts:

    The Great Red spot is a storm that has lasted more than 300 years.

    The storm itself is larger than Earth.

    Lightning on Jupiter is 10 times stronger than lightning on Earth.

15

16

The Asteroid belt??? I'm gonna need some help getting through this silly maze!
Can you help Pavo find his way through the asteroid belt to Mars?

Asteroid Explorer Facts:

There are more than 1.5 million asteroids in the Asteroid belt.

Asteroids are also considered minor planets or planetoids.

"ROVER" "Hmmmm Rover? That's a silly looking dog! Maybe there are humans on Mars too! Do you see any humans?"

Mars Explorer Facts:

Mars is half the size of Earth and has 2 Moons.

Mars has the Largest Volcano in the solar system called Olympus Mons. It is 3 times larger than Mount Everest.

Mars also has a canyon 2,800 miles deep. That would be equivalent to driving from L.A. to N.Y.C.

1 year on Mars equals 687 Earth days and one day on Mars equals 24 hours and 37 minutes on Earth.

If you weigh 50 lbs. on Earth you would weigh 18 lbs. on Mars.

Temperatures range from 80 °F to -200 °F.

Good boy Rover! Let me know if you find any humans!

Mars Explorer Facts:

Rover Curiosity is an automated motor vehicle that propels itself across the surface of Mars.

Rover travels 660 feet a day and runs off a small generator that will last up to 23 months.

Rovers job is to collect rock and soil samples of the Mars surface.

"Next stop Earth!! Can't wait to finally prove that humans exist!"
On the way to earth I fly by its gray and gloomy moon.

The moon is over 225,000 miles away from the earth.

If you weigh 50 lbs. on Earth you would weigh 8 lbs. on our moon.

The earth's moon orbits the earth every 27 earth days.

The first man to walk on the moon was Neil Armstrong on July 20, 1969.

Earth's Moon is the 5th largest moon in the Solar System.

The Moon's gravitational influence produces the ocean tides.

My book "Attack of the Humans" said that surely there would be a human on Earth but it's hot and all I see is sand. Maybe Venus will be a little better living conditions!

Earth Explorer Facts:

Earth is 30% land and 70% water.

The name Earth has been around for about 1,000 years and means "the ground".

If you weigh 50lbs. on Earth you would weigh 50 lbs. on Earth.... Duh!

I was wrong! Being stuck in a volcano on Venus is much worse!

Say, "GO PAVO GO!" And help Pavo get out of the volcano.

Venus Explorer Facts:

 Venus has more volcanoes than any other planet.

 Venus rotates in a direction opposite than Earth's rotation.

 If you weigh 50 lbs. on Earth you would weigh 45 lbs. on Venus.

 1 days equals 243 Earth day and one year equals 225 Earth years.

"Wahooooooooooooo!!!"

25

Mercury is the closest planet to the Sun, one minute I'm working on my tan the next I'm an alien popcicle!

Mercury Explorer Facts:

One side of Mercury is 800 degrees F while the other side is -300 °F.

Mercury is a little larger than Earths moon.

If you weigh 50 lbs. on Earth you would weigh 18 lbs. on Mercury.

1 day on Mercury equals 176 Earth days and 1 year equals 88 Earth Days.

Yay the Sun!!!

Sun Explorer Fact:

   The Sun is about 5 billion years old.

   The Earth can fit in the Sun over a million times.

   If you weigh 50 lbs. on Earth you would weigh 1,353 lbs. and be burnt to a crisp on the Sun.

YOWZA it's hot! Thank you for helping me explore the Solar System!

Can you name all of the planets Pavo visited on his trip?

Websites cited:

Exploratorium.com, kidsastronomy.com

*science.nationalgeographic.com/science/space/**solar-system**/, **solarsystem**.nasa.gov/, nineplanets.org, exploratorium.com*

http://www.livedash.com/transcript/into_the_universe_with_stephen_hawking-(the_story_of_everything)/6222/DSCP/Sunday_May_02_2010/282433/

http://www.space-explorers.com/internal/gemini/?forum=opcorner&post=786

http://www.wallscorner.com/view-nasa__neptune-1024x768.html

http://imgsrc.hubblesite.org/hu/db/images/hs-2007-32-b-full_jpg.jpg

http://nssdc.gsfc.nasa.gov/image/planetary/saturn/saturn.jpg

http://imgsrc.hubblesite.org/hu/db/images/hs-2008-42-a-full_jpg.jpg

http://imgsrc.hubblesite.org/hu/db/images/hs-2008-27-c-full_jpg.jpg

http://phys.org/news146762346.html

http://marsrover.nasa.gov/gallery/artwork/roving_br.html

http://idahobusinessreview.com/files/2010/05/mars-rover.jpg

http://photojournal.jpl.nasa.gov/jpegMod/PIA00106_modest.jpg

http://photojournal.jpl.nasa.gov/jpegMod/PIA00104_modest.jpg

http://www.jpl.nasa.gov/images/stars/skymorph-browse.jpg

A note from the author:

I wrote *Pavo Explores The Solar System* because my son and I love to learn about the universe and how it works. When I tried to find him books I noticed there weren't many to choose from which met our needs. Some were either fun with little to no information, or had lots of information but not much fun for my little one to read. To meet the needs of my child I created Pavo. I am sure your child will enjoy the combination of fun reading and interesting facts as Pavo takes you on a tour of our solar system.

For additional information about Dana or Pavo feel free to visit www.pavoexploresthesolarsystem.com

Dana Rowe

Notes And Your Drawing

Notes And Your Drawing